How far is it to the moon?

Disney BOOKS BY MAIL

DK Direct Limited
Managing Art Editor Eljay Crompton
Senior Editor Rosemary McCormick
Writer Alexandra Parsons
Illustrators The Alvin White Studios and Richard Manning
Designers Amanda Barlow, Wayne Blades, Veneta Bullen,
Richard Clemson, Sarah Goodwin, Diane Klein, Sonia Whillock

Contents

How did explorers know which way to go?

By watching the position of the sun in the sky during the day and the stars at night. They knew that the sun always rises in the east and sets in the west. They also knew the position of the stars and the patterns they make. So when they looked up into the sky, the sun or the stars told them where they were.

Where am I?

Seven hundred years ago the compass was invented. The arrow in a compass always points north. By seeing where north was, early explorers could then figure out which way south, east, and west were.

Who said that?

Why did the egg go into the jungle?
Because it was an eggsplorer!

Early explorer facts

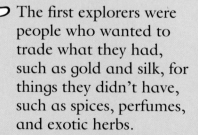

The first explorers were people who wanted to trade what they had, such as gold and silk, for things they didn't have, such as spices, perfumes, and exotic herbs.

W ho were the first people to sail around the world?

A group of Spanish and Portuguese sailors led by their captain, Ferdinand Magellan. They left Spain on September 20, 1519 with 270 men, five ships, 23 charts, and six compasses. They arrived home three years later, with just 17 men and one leaking ship.

Lonesome trail

The first person to sail around the world alone was an American. His name was Captain Joshua Slocum. Captain Slocum began his trip from Boston in 1895, and arrived back home three years later.

Where did you get that name?

Magellan named the Pacific Ocean *Mar Pacifico*, which means "calm ocean" in English.

Food for thought

 Magellan and his crew ran out of food, such as salted meat and vegetables, on the long journey across the Pacific. All they had to eat were biscuits. So if you're planning to sail around the world, pack a BIG picnic basket!

Who was Christopher Columbus?

He was the first European explorer to bring knowledge of America back to Europe. He wasn't trying to find America, though, he was trying to find a new sea route to India. No one knows for sure just where he landed, but they do know when – 1492. He was so sure he was in India, that he even named the people there Indians.

A rhyme to help you remember
In fourteen hundred and ninety-two, Columbus sailed the ocean blue.

Christopher Columbus
Here is Mr. Columbus looking very important. For his journey he was given three ships by Queen Isabella and King Ferdinand of Spain – the Niña, the Pinta, and the Santa Maria.

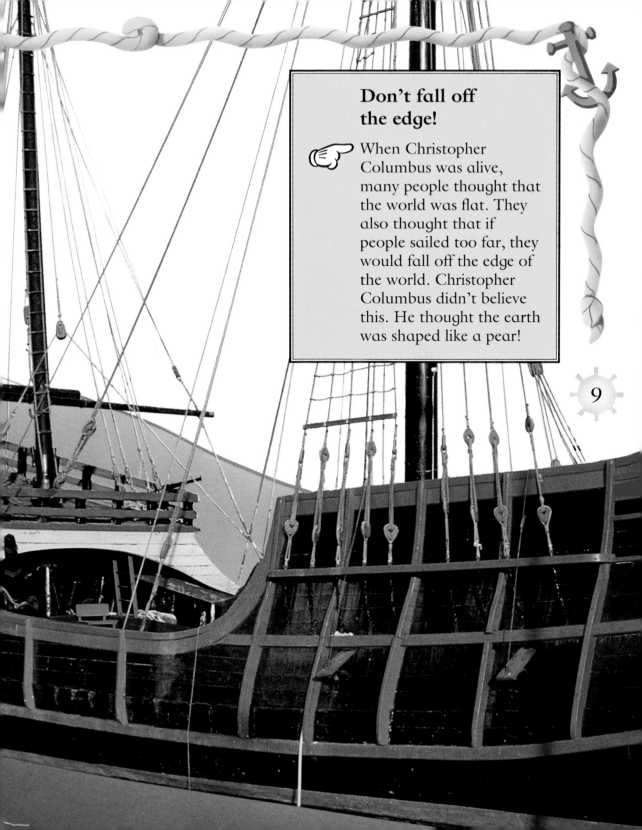

Don't fall off the edge!

☞ When Christopher Columbus was alive, many people thought that the world was flat. They also thought that if people sailed too far, they would fall off the edge of the world. Christopher Columbus didn't believe this. He thought the earth was shaped like a pear!

9

Were there any lady explorers?

Long ago, women weren't given much chance to do exciting things like exploring, but that didn't stop them from trying. Many famous lady explorers were able to discover how people from other countries lived.

A very brave lady
Mary Kingsley was an explorer who traveled alone from England to Africa over a hundred years ago.

High flyer
Amelia Earhart was a famous lady pilot. She set many flying records. She disappeared mysteriously over the Pacific Ocean in 1937.

First ladies

In 1767, a French girl named Jeanne Baret became the first woman to sail around the world. She dressed up as a man to trick the captain into letting her work on the ship.

In 1930, Amy Johnson became the first woman to fly alone from Europe to Australia. She took a gun, a mosquito net, a sun hat, a parachute, and some sandwiches. She flew 10,000 miles in 19 days.

Why is it so hard to climb high mountains?

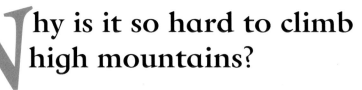

Because mountains have steep, icy, slippery slopes. Also, falling snow could hurt climbers, or even bury them. There are strong winds, too. And, the higher up you go, the less oxygen there is, which makes it harder to breathe.

12

Mountain humor
Do mountains have ears?
Yes, they have mountaineers!

The highest mountain in the world!

In 1953, Edmund Hillary from New Zealand and Tenzing Norgay from Nepal became the first people to climb Mount Everest. Everest is five and a half miles high. Edmund Hillary took this picture of Tenzing on the mountain top.

Mighty mountain facts

When lots of snow or ice suddenly fall down a mountain, it's called an avalanche. Avalanches often happen in spring when the snow starts to melt.

Are there places on Earth where no one has been?

Yes. There are thousands of square miles beneath the ocean that have never been explored because it is too deep and too dangerous. There are some parts of the ocean that are six and a half miles deep. If you put the highest mountain in the world, Mount Everest, in the ocean, the top would still be a mile under water!

Mountains to climb
There are some mountains in far-off countries like Tibet that have never been climbed.

Don't forget the map!
There are maps of the ocean floor just as there are maps of dry land. The floor beneath the ocean is just as uneven as the earth's land surface. There are high mountains, deep valleys, and fiery volcanoes.

Underwater living

☞ The first underwater home was built on the bottom of the Red Sea in the Middle East. Five men spent a month there.

☞ There's an underwater hotel in Key Largo, Florida, where you see fish swimming past your bedroom window. It's 30 feet under water and you have to scuba dive to the main door.

15

What would happen if you kept on digging a hole?

You would end up very tired and hot, and ruin your shovel! That's because it's impossible to dig right through the earth. Under the soil and sea and sand are layers of rock too hard to dig or cut through.

Keep digging
The deepest anyone has ever dug or drilled is six miles.

16

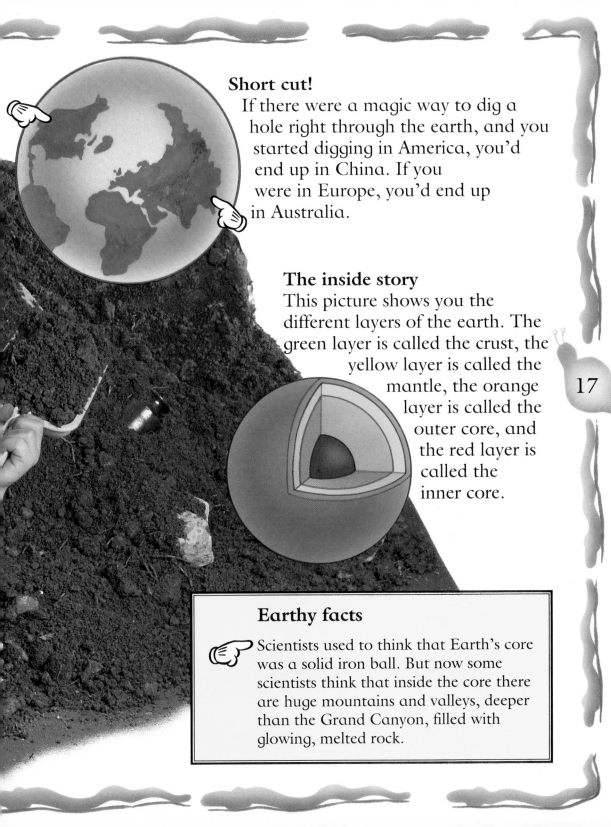

Short cut!
If there were a magic way to dig a hole right through the earth, and you started digging in America, you'd end up in China. If you were in Europe, you'd end up in Australia.

The inside story
This picture shows you the different layers of the earth. The green layer is called the crust, the yellow layer is called the mantle, the orange layer is called the outer core, and the red layer is called the inner core.

17

Earthy facts
Scientists used to think that Earth's core was a solid iron ball. But now some scientists think that inside the core there are huge mountains and valleys, deeper than the Grand Canyon, filled with glowing, melted rock.

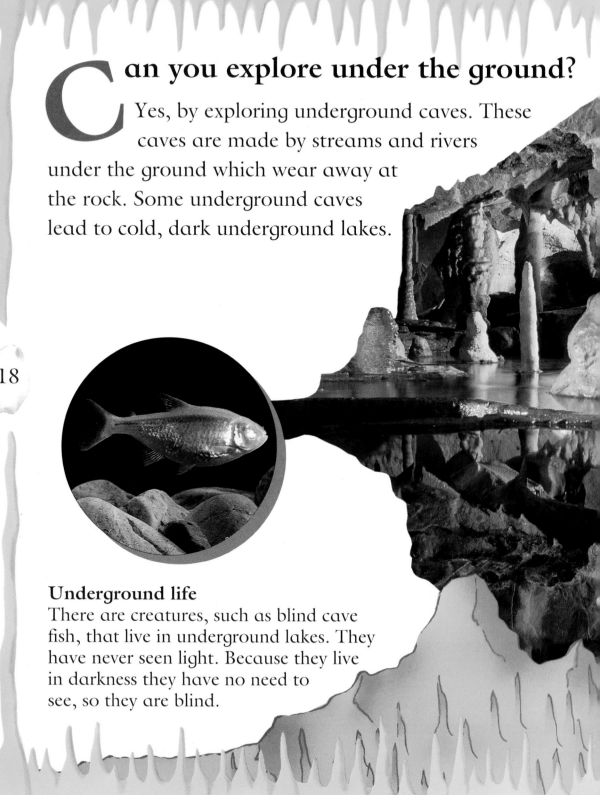

Can you explore under the ground?

Yes, by exploring underground caves. These caves are made by streams and rivers under the ground which wear away at the rock. Some underground caves lead to cold, dark underground lakes.

Underground life

There are creatures, such as blind cave fish, that live in underground lakes. They have never seen light. Because they live in darkness they have no need to see, so they are blind.

Deep, dark cave facts

☞ Lechuguilla Cave, in New Mexico, is America's deepest cave. It is 1,565 feet deep. The largest part of the cave is 600 feet long and 200 feet high. It is called the most beautiful cave in the world. To get into the cave you have to climb down a rope into a 70-foot pit!

How do you explore under the ocean?

In water that isn't very deep, all you need is a snorkel and a mask. A snorkel is a hollow tube that goes from your mouth through the water up to the air. To go deeper you need a tank of air. But to go really deep, you need a submarine.

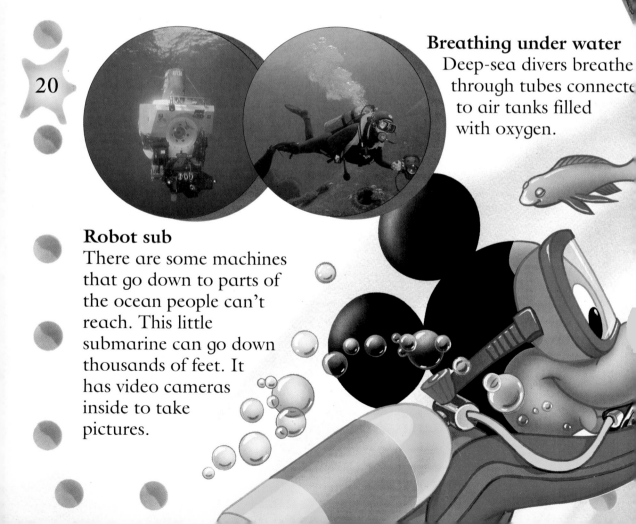

Breathing under water
Deep-sea divers breathe through tubes connecte to air tanks filled with oxygen.

Robot sub
There are some machines that go down to parts of the ocean people can't reach. This little submarine can go down thousands of feet. It has video cameras inside to take pictures.

Deep sea gags
What bank robber lives
at the bottom of the ocean?
Billy the Squid.

Deep sea facts

☞ There are a lot of sunken ships on the ocean floor. Divers sometimes find treasure on board.

☞ Submarines have big tanks which are filled with water to weigh the sub down so it can sink. Tanks filled with air push the water out when it's time to go back up.

How far is it to the moon?

It's 239,000 miles from Earth. The journey would take almost three weeks in a jumbo jet. If you walked it would take you seven years. Make sure you wear comfortable shoes!

22

Moon matter
The moon is made of rocks and dust. There is no water or air. It gets boiling hot when the sun shines during the day, and freezing cold at night.

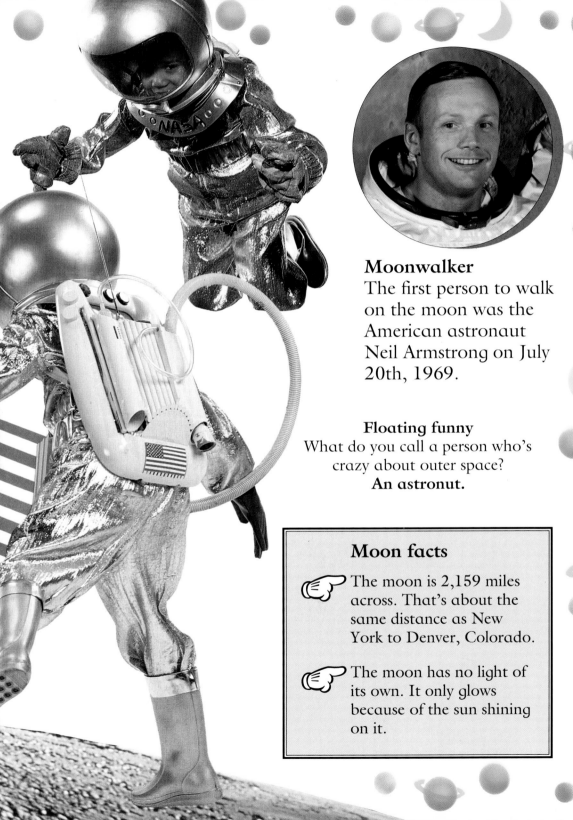

Moonwalker
The first person to walk on the moon was the American astronaut Neil Armstrong on July 20th, 1969.

Floating funny
What do you call a person who's crazy about outer space?
An astronut.

Moon facts

 The moon is 2,159 miles across. That's about the same distance as New York to Denver, Colorado.

The moon has no light of its own. It only glows because of the sun shining on it.

W hat's it like inside a space shuttle?

It's a cross between an airplane and a space hotel. Astronauts live up in space for months, doing experiments, checking satellites, and looking at stars. Because there's no gravity in space – and without gravity things are weightless and float around – astronauts often do their work floating upside down!

Space food
Astronauts' food is put into specially sealed packages.

Everyday life in space

☞ When male astronauts shave, they use special razors that suck in the hairs like vacuum cleaners. Otherwise their whiskers would float around forever.

☞ Food that is eaten in space is made extra-sticky so it stays on the fork!

A spacey kind of joke!
When do astronauts eat their food?
At launch time!

Could people live on Mars?

Absolutely not! There's no oxygen to breathe and the sky is full of swirling red dust. There's no rain, and no food. It would also be much too cold for comfort. When you think about it, it's best to stay home.

Space snapshots
These pictures of Mars were taken from the spacecraft Voyager, which did not have people on board, just special cameras. You can see just how lumpy and bumpy the surface of the planet is.

The red planet

Mars is a small, dry planet. On a very clear night, you can just about see a red glow in the sky – that's Mars.

Mars facts

☞ Mars is half the size of Earth.

☞ There's a volcano on Mars that's 15 miles high – nearly three times higher than Mount Everest.

☞ Before we were able to photograph Mars closely, people used to believe that there was life on Mars. But now scientists know that because of poisonous gases, nothing could live there.

MICKEY'S Mind teaser

Match each clue to the picture it describes.

1. It's lumpy and bumpy with lots of red dust.

2. It's like a hotel and an airplane rolled into one.

3. They're very big, and hard to climb.

4. He was given three ships to use on his trip.

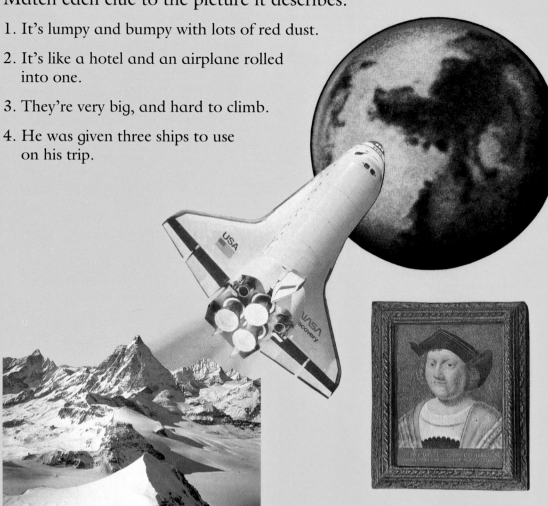

Answers: 1. Mars; 2. A space shuttle;
3. mountains; 4. Christopher Columbus.